Cool Careers in Science

▸ Designing tomorrow's games

▸ How games are designed

▸ The future of games and apps

Computer
GAME & APP
Developers

ALTERNATIVE REALITY DEVELOPERS

ARTIFICIAL INTELLIGENCE SCIENTISTS

COMPUTER GAME & APP DEVELOPERS

DRIVERLESS VEHICLE DEVELOPERS

DRONE PILOTS

ENTERTAINMENT ENGINEERS

FORENSIC SCIENTISTS

PROFESSIONAL HACKERS

RENEWABLE ENERGY WORKERS

ROBOTICS DEVELOPERS

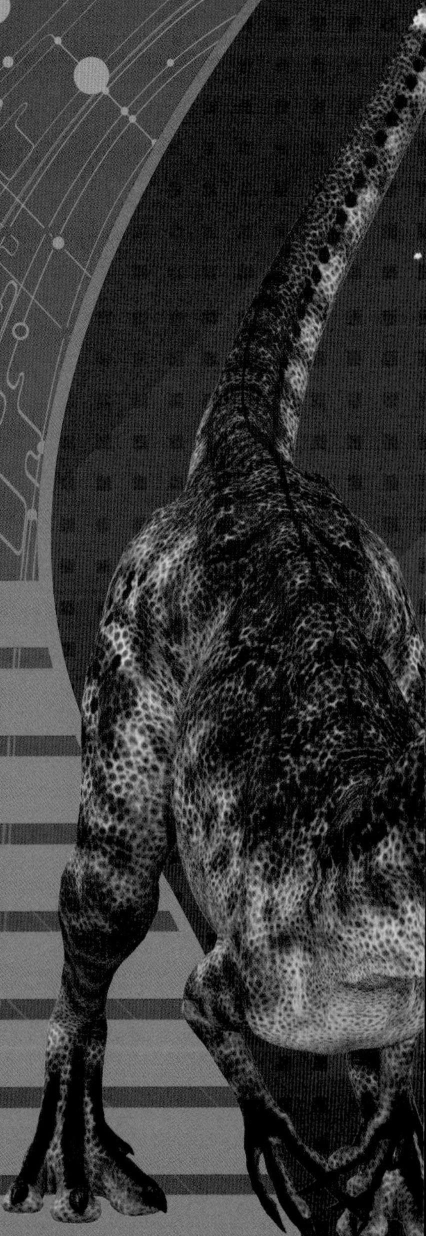

Cool Careers
in Science

Computer
GAME & APP
Developers

ANDREW MORKES

MC

MASON CREST
PHILADELPHIA
MIAMI

Mason Crest
450 Parkway Drive, Suite D
Broomall, Pennsylvania 19008
(866) MCP-BOOK (toll-free)

First printing

9 8 7 6 5 4 3 2 1

HARDBACK ISBN: 978-1-4222-4295-7
SERIES ISBN: 978-1-4222-4292-6
EBOOK ISBN: 978-1-4222-7512-2

Cataloging-in-Publication Data on file with the Library of Congress

Developed and Produced by National Highlights, Inc.
Interior and cover design: Jana Rade, impact studios
Interior layout: Annalisa Gumbrecht, Studio Gumbrecht
Production: Michelle Luke
Proofreader: Susan Uttendorfsky

QR CODES AND LINKS TO THIRD-PARTY CONTENT

Table of Contents

KEY ICONS TO LOOK FOR:

WORDS TO UNDERSTAND: These words with their easy-to-understand definitions will increase the reader's understanding of the text while building vocabulary skills.

SIDEBARS: This boxed material within the main text allows readers to build knowledge, gain insights, explore possibilities, and broaden their perspectives by weaving together additional information to provide realistic and holistic perspectives.

EDUCATIONAL VIDEOS: Readers can view videos by scanning our QR codes, providing them with additional educational content to supplement the text. Examples include news coverage, moments in history, speeches, iconic sports moments, and much more!

TEXT-DEPENDENT QUESTIONS: These questions send the reader back to the text for more careful attention to the evidence presented there.

RESEARCH PROJECTS: Readers are pointed toward areas of further inquiry connected to each chapter. Suggestions are provided for projects that encourage deeper research and analysis.

CAREERS IN SCIENCE OFFER GOOD PAY, THE OPPORTUNITY TO HELP PEOPLE, AND OTHER REWARDS

Where would we be without science? Well, we'd be without computers, smartphones, and other cutting-edge technologies. Crimes would take longer to solve without modern forensic analysis techniques. More of our private information would be stolen by hackers. We'd be stuck relying on environmentally unfriendly fossil fuels instead of using renewable energy. And life would be less fun because we wouldn't have drones; awe-inspiring and physics-defying roller coasters; the apps that we use to help us to stay fit, find directions, and get the news; and the computer and video games that we play for hours and hours.

Job markets are sometimes strong and sometimes weak, but a career in science (which, for the purposes of this series, includes the related fields of technology and engineering) is almost a sure path to a comfortable life. The following paragraphs provide more information on why a career in science is a great choice.

Good pay. People in science careers earn some of the highest salaries in the work world. Median annual salaries for those in computer and mathematical careers in the United States are $84,575, according to the U.S. Department of Labor (USDL). This is much higher than the median earnings ($37,690) for all careers. Additionally, those in life, physical, and social science occupations can earn $64,510, and those in engineering careers earn $79,180. Science professionals who become managers or who launch their own businesses can earn anywhere from $150,000 to $300,000 or more.

Strong employment prospects. There are shortages of science workers throughout the world, according to the consulting firm ManpowerGroup. In fact, engineering workers are the third most in demand occupational field in the world. Technicians rank fourth, and computer and information technology professionals rank sixth.

There's a shortage of software engineers in more than twenty countries, including in the United States, Canada, Mexico, Japan, and the United Kingdom, according to the recruitment firm Michael Page. Other science careers where there is a shortage of workers include electronics engineers (nineteen countries), electrical engineers (sixteen countries), data analysts (eleven countries), and hardware engineers (six countries), among other workers.

The USDL predicts that employment of computer and information technology professionals in the United States will grow by 13 percent during the next decade. Career opportunities for those in life, physical, and social science occupations will grow by 10 percent. Both of these career fields are growing faster than the average for all careers. The outlook is also good for engineering professionals. Employment is expected to grow by 7 percent during the next decade. The strongest opportunities will be found in renewable energy and robotics.

By 2026, the USDL predicts that there will be more than 876,000 new jobs in science, technology, engineering, and mathematics fields.

Rewarding work environment and many career options. A career in science is fulfilling because you get to use both your creative and practical sides to develop new technologies (or improve existing ones), solve problems, and make the world a better place. There's a common misconception that science workers spend most of their time in dreary, windowless laboratories or offices. While they do spend lots of time in the laboratory or offices, they also spend time in the field, testing, troubleshooting, and trying out their inventions or discoveries. Some science professionals launch their own businesses, which can be both fun and very rewarding.

Job opportunities are available throughout the United States and the world. Science professionals play such an important role in our modern world that there are jobs almost anywhere, although many positions are found in big cities.

IS A CAREER IN SCIENCE RIGHT FOR ME?

Test your interest. How many of these statements do you agree with?

_____ My favorite classes in school are computer- and science-related.

_____ I am interested in design, art, and other creative fields.

_____ I like to learn about scientific breakthroughs.

_____ I like to use technology to solve problems.

_____ I like to build and fix things.

_____ I enjoy doing science experiments.

_____ I am curious about how things work.

_____ I like to invent things.

_____ I have a good imagination.

_____ I like to build electronics and other things that require electricity.

_____ I am good at math.

If many of the statements above describe you, then you should consider a career in the sciences. But you don't need to select a career right now. Check out this book on a career as a computer game and app developer, and other books in the series, to learn more about occupational paths in the sciences and related fields. Good luck with your career exploration!

WORDS TO UNDERSTAND

augmented reality: a computer-generated system that combines a virtual environment with imaginary elements that are introduced to a real environment; examples include Snapchat lenses and the game *Pokémon Go*

congressional district: in the United States, an area that contains a large group of voters that elect members of the U.S. House of Representatives; there are 435 congressional districts in the United States

virtual reality: a computer-generated experience that takes place within a simulated environment using headgear or other equipment that shuts out the real world

wearable technology: devices that people wear that use smart sensors and an internet connection; they gather information and help people become healthier, better manage time, or meet other life goals, and they enhance the gaming experience; examples include smartwatches, fitness trackers, head-mounted displays, and smart clothing and jewelry

Chapter 1

WHAT DO COMPUTER GAME AND APP DEVELOPERS DO?

COMPUTER GAMES AND APPS

Unless you've been grounded from using technology your entire life, you already know all about computer games and apps. But if you don't, let's discuss them.

COMPUTER GAMES

Computer games are played on video game consoles, computers, arcade consoles, and smartphones and other mobile computing devices. Games can be played by connecting a cartridge to a game console, by downloading software onto a digital device, by playing games that have been inserted into a game console at the factory, by using **virtual reality** or **augmented reality** devices, or by visiting gaming websites. In addition to being played for the purposes of entertainment, computer games are also used in corporate and military training, health care, education, science, and other

A teen plays an online computer game.

settings. Computer games are extremely popular. Sixty-four percent of Americans own a device that they use to play computer games, according to the Entertainment Software Association (ESA). In 2017, Americans spent a whopping $29.1 billion on video game content, up from $17.5 billion in 2010.

The computer game industry provides many jobs. There are more than 2,710 video game company locations (meaning some companies have more than one office) across 84 percent of the **congressional districts** in the United States, according to the ESA. Approximately 220,000 people work in the U.S. computer gaming industry. Additionally, hundreds of thousands of other game workers are employed at companies around the world. Some gaming professionals are self-employed. This means that they work for themselves instead of for a company or other organization. They develop and sell their games, or are hired by companies and other employers to do development work part time.

APPS

An app is software that is designed to perform a specific task. It is also known as an "application." Apps help us save time and complete tasks more efficiently. You use apps when you post a photo on Instagram, play games on the internet, get the news, text your friends, get directions to a party, and perform a variety of other tasks. Apps are available in dozens of categories, but the most popular interest areas are games, business, education, lifestyle, entertainment, utilities, travel, health and fitness, and food and drink.

Desktop apps are used to perform tasks on desktop or laptop computers. Examples of desktop apps include Microsoft Office applications (Word, Excel, etc.), web browsers (Google Chrome, Mozilla Firefox, Microsoft Edge, and Explorer), and Adobe Photoshop.

Many developers create apps for smartphones and other mobile devices.

Mobile apps perform functions on mobile devices such as smartphones (Apple iPhone, Google Android, etc.), tablet computers, e-readers, **wearable technology**, and other handheld or wearable internet-enabled telecommunications/computing devices.

Apps are very popular. As of March 2017, there were 2.8 million apps available for download at the Google Play store and 2.2 million apps available in the Apple's App Store, according to Statista.com.

More than 1.6 million software developers and programmers are employed in the United States, according to the U.S. Department of Labor. Glance, an app developer, reports that about 19 million people worldwide are software developers, with 8.7 million of this group specializing in mobile apps. About 33 percent of all software developers work in Asia, 29.7 percent work in Europe, and 29.4 percent are employed in the United States and Canada.

Learn what daily life is like for a video game designer

A game developer works on level designs.

COMPUTER GAME DEVELOPERS

Game developers design, write, program, animate, and test computer games. At large companies, they typically specialize in one of these tasks and may be known as game designers and engineers, game programmers, game authors, game composers, game artists, etc. Developers who are self-employed and those who work at small companies perform all these tasks and many others (marketing, sales, etc.) to develop and sell games. To make it even more confusing, some companies may describe those who work on the creative side of video games as game designers, and those who write the computer code that allows the game to be played as game developers or game programmers. For the purposes of this book, game developers are those who work both on the creative and the technical aspects of games.

Game developers perform the following tasks:

- Develop ideas for games that entertain, educate, or perform other functions

- Develop game plots and characters, including storylines and character biographies, because it's very important that the main characters are both visually appealing and interesting

- Imagine and develop the visual look of the game—what the main characters wear, how the weapons or tools used in the game look, and the appearance of the backgrounds in various levels

- Create a game design document, which provides information on what their game is about and why it's worth making; it also provides information on its characters, plot, and other features for coworkers and company management

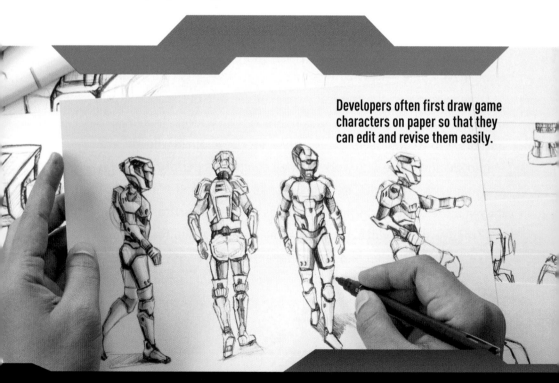

Developers often first draw game characters on paper so that they can edit and revise them easily.

- Create a storyboard: a type of roadmap that describes the order of the screens/features that users will see on the main levels or stages of a computer game

- Write the computer code (C++, C#, Python, Perl, and JavaScript are popular programming languages in the gaming industry) that converts the designs into a game; some developers use video game development software such as DarkBASIC Pro, GameMaker, Game Editor, Adventure Game Studio, GDevelop, and Tiled

- Perform code reviews to ensure that the code does what it has been designed to do in the game

- Use computer software to create the music and sound effects for the game; this is important because users quickly lose interest in games with poor sound quality or unbelievable or annoying sound effects

- Create special effects such as explosions or volcano eruptions

- Develop the user design interface (both software and hardware) that allows the gamer to easily use the game and have an enjoyable experience

- Work closely with programmers, artists, sound designers, company management, and others during the development process

- Repeatedly test the game, identify and document where problems occurred, fix the issues, and recheck the game to determine if it is functioning correctly

- Organize blind testing events in which average users are asked to playtest the game before its release; this allows them to identify any usability issues or bugs that were missed by game testers

A game development firm owner will perform the above duties and many others, such as:

- Hiring, training, managing, and firing (if necessary) staff
- Managing company finances
- Preparing pitches for game publishers to try to convince them to fund or produce their game
- Attending industry conferences to learn about the latest game development trends and promote their products
- Working with marketing professionals to develop print, online (including on social media), and broadcast advertising campaigns for their products

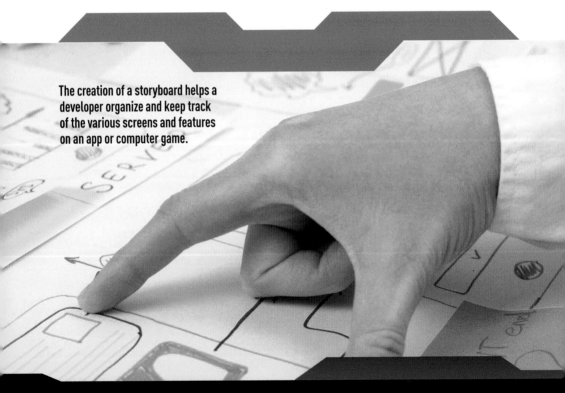

The creation of a storyboard helps a developer organize and keep track of the various screens and features on an app or computer game.

DAY IN THE LIFE: GAME DEVELOPER

People often tell me that I have a dream job, and I can't disagree. I'm a lead developer at a game development company in Seattle, Washington, that produces massively multiplayer online sports games. Sometimes I do think I'm dreaming because I get to turn my creative ideas into video games; I work with some cool and creative people; and my company offers free lunches, yoga classes on site, and a game room with vintage arcade games to blow off steam.

Every day is different. As lead developer, I oversee the work of all the developers—thirty to forty in all. These developers are working on everything from game art and characters to script writing and level design, to audio, programming, and anything else that's involved with making a game. I always push my developers to turn something that's good into something better. Because, after all, there are a lot of good games, but only a select few games make it to the "this game is awesome!" level.

I spend a lot of time meeting with the other lead developers to make sure that every department has what it needs to get projects done. Staying on schedule is vital because while we're toiling over the design and programming aspects of the product, the sales and marketing staff are working hard to promote the product in advance of its sale to the public. To keep us on schedule, I occasionally pitch in, creating storyboards, doing alpha testing, and whatever else is needed.

Other than office perks and the opportunity to work with some really fun and talented people, I really like that I can turn an idea that occurred to me while I watched a baseball, soccer, or football game into a finished product just six months later (of course, work on every game does not go smoothly). At one time, hundreds of thousands of people all over the world are having fun playing a game that I helped to create. How cool is that?!

APP DEVELOPERS

Whether they're creating a desktop app or a mobile one, applications developers begin their work by asking a series of questions:

- What is the goal of this application?
- Who is the target audience?
- Will this be a desktop or mobile app?
- How will photos, animation, videos, colors, and design elements be used?
- Will it be a free or fee-based product?
- Who are your competitors?
- What features (inclusion of foreign languages, incorporation of geo-location services, connection to the Internet of Things, etc.) would you like the app to include?
- How much will it cost to develop the app?

An app developer writes code on a glass idea wall while working on a new software program.

- What platform (iOS, Android, etc.) will the app be created for?
- What are the cybersecurity concerns associated with the application?
- What is your deadline?
- What is your budget?

DEVELOPER CAREER PATH

If you are highly skilled and work hard, you can advance to a position in management, or even start a business. Here is a typical career ladder for computer game and app developers:

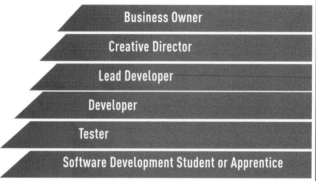

Business Owner

Creative Director

Lead Developer

Developer

Tester

Software Development Student or Apprentice

An app developer discusses his work

Receiving detailed answers to these and other questions is extremely important because app development can be time-consuming and expensive. According to Clearbridge Mobile, a specialized mobile app development company, it costs $75,000 to $150,000 to create a small app, $150,00 to $250,000 to build a medium-sized app, and more than $250,000 to develop a large-scale app.

Next, the applications developer does the following:

- Creates a wireframe: a guide that presents the proposed content, functions, and structure of an app; it allows developers to see how the various components interact, as well as how users will interact with various features, without having to build the app

- Creates a storyboard: a type of roadmap that describes the order of the screens/features that users will see on the app

- Develops the program architecture and design strategy

- Builds and tests the prototype: an unfinished version of the app that is ready to be tested and modified

- Tests the program to identify and correct bugs and errors

- Repeats the testing process (including blind testing, in which average users are asked to use the app) to ensure that there are no issues and that the app is easy to use

TEST THE WATERS BY BECOMING A GAME OR APP TESTER

Many aspiring computer game and app developers choose to explore their interest in these fields by becoming game or app testers. Working as a tester allows you to learn the business from the ground up. You'll get a chance to test exciting, well-designed games and apps, and those that are kind of boring or full of bugs and other errors. By seeing various levels of quality, you'll learn what makes a well-designed game or app. Many game and app developers first broke into the industry as testers.

As a tester, you'll assess the game or app's installation (how to download or otherwise install it), functionality (how it works), network performance (how it works with other products), playability, and other concerns. You'll look for coding errors and other problems that affect the product's performance. Once you identify issues, you'll write a report that identifies the problem, describe in detail where in the game or app it occurred, and what you were doing in the product when the problem arose (i.e., the exact combinations of controller movements, keystrokes, and mouse clicks that caused the problem). Testers play games or use apps for long periods of time, trying to get the product to crash. It's better to catch issues before the product's launch, rather than when it's in the hands of users.

Game development firms have very casual dress codes.

WORK ENVIRONMENT

Computer game and app developers work in comfortable offices, with good lighting, a climate-controlled environment, and access to cutting-edge technology. Some developers may be allowed to work remotely, which means that instead of going to an office, they can work from their home, a coffee shop, or other remote location. Developers may occasionally need to travel to the offices of current or potential clients, as well as to industry conferences.

Game and app design is a deadline-driven business, and developers must be willing to work extra hours when necessary. While there will be times when you work a standard forty-hour week (Monday through Friday, 9:00 a.m. to 5:00 p.m.), there will be many instances when you work much longer hours to get the job done.

Computer game and app developers spend a lot of time working at their computers. This work can cause eyestrain, general fatigue (tiredness), muscle strains, and carpal tunnel syndrome (pain, numbness, and tingling in the hands and arms). Developers can prevent or reduce the reduce the effects of these potential issues by taking frequent breaks from the computer and gaming equipment and using ergonomic chairs, keyboards, and other office equipment.

Ergonomics is a field in which scientists study anthropometry (body sizes, shapes, etc.), biomechanics (muscles, forces, etc.), environmental physics (light, heat, cold, noise, etc.), and applied and social psychology (communication, learning, behaviors, etc.) to create human-friendly environments, furniture, equipment, and machinery.

The dress code in the computer game and app development industry is very casual. Managers are much more concerned that a developer has top-notch design and programming skills than with what they wear to work.

TEXT-DEPENDENT QUESTIONS:

1. How many people work in the U.S. computer game industry?
2. What are some duties of a computer game business owner?
3. What is a wireframe?

RESEARCH PROJECT:

Learn more about the differences between desktop and mobile apps. What are the pros and cons of each format, and what challenges do developers face when working on them? Write a report that provides more information on each, and present your findings to your computer class.

Chapter 2

TERMS OF THE TRADE

action games: Those in which the player is in control and is at the center of game action.

action-adventure games: Those that involve completing game-long quests and/or overcoming obstacles to reach a series of goals, or a main goal. These games often feature puzzle- and riddle-solving and fighting sequences.

actions: In a computer game, the way in which an object reacts to input or interacts with other objects.

adventure games: Those in which the player must interact with other characters and game elements to solve challenges and reach a goal.

alpha testing: The process of testing a computer game or app while it is still in the development phase.

app: Software that is designed to perform specific tasks. Desktop applications are used to perform tasks on desktop or laptop computers. Mobile apps perform functions on mobile devices such as smartphones (Apple iPhone,

Google Android, etc.) and other handheld or wearable internet-enabled telecommunications/computing devices. Apps may also be known as **applications**.

artificial intelligence: The simulation of human intelligence by machinery and computer systems.

active object: An object—such as a character, weapon, hill, or doorway—that a player can interact with in a game.

active sounds: Sounds that are linked to a player's actions in a game.

app engine: The programming platform that is used to create and run an app.

application programming interface: A computer game and app development tool that allows for a connection between one function (operating system, service, or app) and another.

augmented reality: A computer-generated system that combines a virtual environment with imaginary elements that are introduced to a real environment; examples include Snapchat lenses and the game *Pokémon Go*.

avatar: The online representation, or persona, of a game player.

backend code: The code for an app that runs on databases and a server (on site, or in the cloud) and that powers everything that the user does with an app.

background music: Music that sets the mood of a game level. It is not generated by a player's actions.

background object: A component in the game frame that the player can see, but cannot interact with.

beta testing: The process of testing a computer game or app right before it will be released to users. Any glitches, bugs, or other issues that are discovered will be fixed before the release of the product.

blind testing: The process in which average users are asked to playtest a computer game or app before its release. This allows developers to identify any usability problems, bugs, or other issues that were missed by game testers.

bug: A glitch or problem with software (basically, a coding error). Some bugs can be exploited by cybercriminals if they are not fixed by the software developer.

bug bounty: Money paid to professional hackers or everyday computer users if they find a bug before the bad guys do.

casual game: A type of video game that provides users with a short and relaxing experience. These games have simple rules and do not require many skills to be able to play. *Asteroids, Bejeweled, Galaga, Space Invaders*, and *Farmville* are examples of casual video games.

casual gamers: Those who play computer games infrequently and who do not necessarily have to win to have an enjoyable experience.

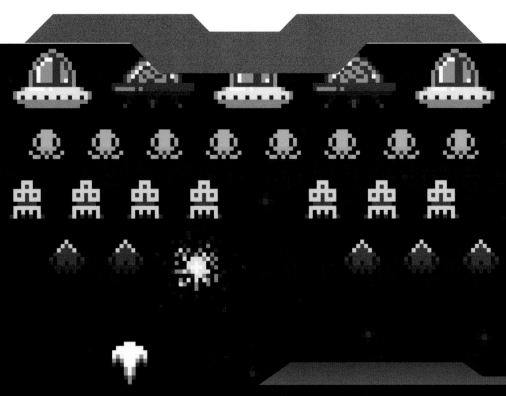

character design document: A summary created by a developer that provides information about a character's appearance, actions, and abilities.

character development: Establishing the characteristics, personality, and abilities of a character.

challenges: Mental or physical challenges that are created by the developer that the player must master to continue in a game or gain rewards.

cloud-based video game: A type of game in which most or all of the technology necessary is located at a cloud computing data center, eliminating the need for the player to buy an expensive game console or a hard copy of the actual game. Cloud-based games are streamed via a high-speed internet connection to the player on a computer, television, or other supported device.

cloud computing: Computer services that are provided over the internet instead of on a personal computer or local server. Sometimes referred to as **the cloud**.

code: Instructions that tell a computer what to do.

concept art: A design that presents the proposed visual look of a character or other object.

concept stage: The first stage of the three-stage production process. In this stage, developers create the main goals of the game, its characters, its look, and other features.

construction stage: The second stage of the three-stage production process. In this stage, developers design and build levels and other components that are needed to play the game.

cooperative games: Those in which players work together to beat the game.

core gamers: Those who play computer games very frequently.

dialogue: What characters say to one another in a video game.

e-sports: Competitive video gaming events in which people of all ages compete against one another live for the chance to win cash prizes.

first-person perspective: A gameplay view in which the player sees the game through the eyes of the character, allowing them to feel as if they are part of the

action. The first-person perspective is used in a variety of gaming genres, but often in role-playing games, adventure games, and driving/racing games.

frontend code: The code (typically HTML, CSS, and JavaScript) in an app that creates the user interface. It is used to create frontend components that include drop-down menus, buttons, sliders, and contact forms. Also known as **client-side programming**.

functionality testing: The process of testing a game or app to see if it operates and delivers the game experience or resources that are intended.

game addiction: A psychological disorder in which the user cannot stop playing video games to the detriment of their health and personal, school, and work lives.

game console: A specialized computer system that allows users to play video games.

game design document: A summary created by a developer that explains what their game is about and why it's worth making. It also provides information on its characters, plot, and other features for programmers and artists.

game engine: The programming platform that is used to create and run a game. Examples include Unity and Unreal.

game frame: What players see in a specific game sequence until they move on to the next area of the game.

game genres: Types of video games; examples include adventure, role-playing, strategy, sports, and fighting. Hybrid games incorporate two or more game genres.

glitch: A sudden malfunction of an app or game that often corrects itself. This makes it hard for developers to identify and fix the problem.

grunts: Slang for low-level, on-screen opponents in a game who are numerous but easily defeated.

hacker: The term for both people who seek to use their computer and hacking skills to do good, and those who use their talents to do bad.

hybrid game genre: One that incorporates two or more game genres.

intellectual property: Creations of the human mind, such as inventions, designs, and artistic and literary works.

Internet of Things: A network of appliances, vehicles, etc., that are embedded with electronics, sensors, software, and other technology that allows them to communicate with each other and share information.

level development: The process of creating settings, stages, locales, or missions in a computer game.

massively multiplayer online game: An interactive game that features up to hundreds of thousands of people playing the same game over the internet at the same time. Some are free, while others require a fee to play.

mobile devices: Smartphones, tablet computers, e-readers, and wearable technology.

mock-up: Visual representations of various components of an app that are created during the design process without having to actually build the app or its underlying functionality.

navigation: The process of moving through a computer game or app.

network: A group of computers that are linked to accomplish a goal.

open-source software: A type of software that is free and which anyone can inspect, modify, and improve the code that makes it work. Some developers use open-source software when creating games and apps.

personal computer gaming: Playing games on a personal computer rather than on a game console.

pitch: A presentation by a developer to a publisher that aims to convince them to produce their game or app or provide funding for development in exchange for a share of the profits once the product is marketed. A pitch that is well-received is typically followed by the preparation of a longer written concept/treatment.

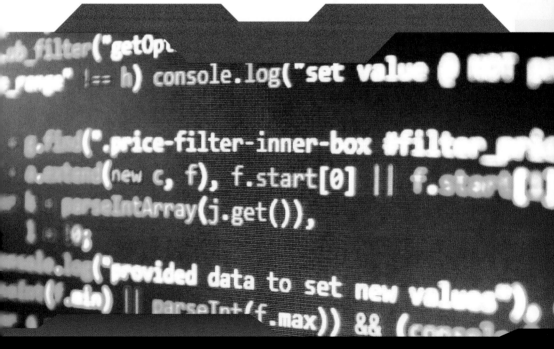

pitch documents: Documents that present or sell a game or app idea to the decision makers at a company.

programming language: Instructions that tell hardware and software what to do; popular programming languages used in the computer game and app industry include C++, C#, and JavaScript. Also called **programming code**.

prototype: An unfinished version of an app or computer game that is ready to be tested and modified.

publishers: Companies that develop, manufacture, and distribute apps and games.

puzzle games: Those that require users to solve a problem or answer a series of questions to continue on to more challenging levels.

role-playing game: A type of computer game genre in which the player takes on the role of a character or characters in a game.

server: A computer that processes requests and delivers data to another computer over a local network or the internet.

shooter game: A computer game genre in which the principal goal is to shoot at one's enemies and otherwise engage in warfare (throwing grenades, fighting with swords, etc.).

simulation games: Those that seek to emulate, or simulate, a real situation or event.

software: A program that operates a computer or allows a user to perform a specific task.

sound effects: Sounds, music, and spoken words that are added to a game to make it more interesting, believable, and fun. Sound effects are also sometimes incorporated into non-game apps.

sports games: Those that simulate real sports such as football, basketball, baseball, golf, soccer, ski racing, pool, darts, and swimming.

SQL: Stands for Structured Query Language; a programming language that is used to store, manipulate, and retrieve data in servers and databases.

storyboard: A type of roadmap that describes the order of the screens/features that users will see on an app, or that describes the main levels or stages of a computer game.

strategy games: Those that require players to use strategies and tactics to overcome challenges.

tester: An individual who tests every aspect of a computer game or app to ensure that it operates properly. May also be known as a **play tester** or **game tester**.

three-dimensional (3-D) game: A computer game that is graphically presented in three dimensions (height, width, and depth). These games feature 3-D characters and 3-D backgrounds.

three-stage production process: The production cycle of a computer game or app with stages of concept, construction, and tuning.

tuning stage: The third stage of the three-stage production process. In this stage, the game is tested for playability and functionality, and revisions are made to address any issues.

two-dimensional (2-D) games: A computer game that is graphically presented in two dimensions (length and width).

user interface: Computer screens and hardware that people use to play a game or use an app. If the user interface is poorly designed, users will become frustrated with the product and will possibly stop using it.

virtual reality: A computer-generated experience that takes place within a simulated environment using headgear or other equipment that shuts out the real world.

virtual world: An imaginary world created in a computer game.

virus: A type of malware that is typically hidden in a software program or computer file; it must be downloaded or forwarded for it to be activated.

voice-overs: Spoken words that are used for dialogue and narration (telling a story and bringing users up to speed on developments) during a computer game.

wearable technology: Devices that people wear that use smart sensors and an internet connection; they enhance the gaming experience or gather information and help people become healthier, better manage time, or meet other life goals. Gaming examples include smart armbands that improve the game experience, video headphones, and Gameband+Minecraft, a wristband that allows users to play the popular game on any computer.

wireframe: A guide that presents the proposed content, functions, and structure of an app. It allows developers to see how the various components interact, as well as how users will interact with various features, without having to build the app.

```
 redrawSiteWithMagic(){
(window).width() < 700){
$('.rotate-left').addClass
$('.rotate-right').addClas
$('.rotate-left').removeCl
$('.rotate-right').removeC
e{

$('.rotate-left-disactivat
$('.rotate-right-disactiva
$('.rotate-left-disactivat
$('.rotate-right-disactiva
```

```
641){
```

WORDS TO UNDERSTAND

bootcamp: a short-term, highly focused learning opportunity in which participants are taught the most important aspects of a complicated topic, such as coding

freelancer: a type of worker who does not work full time for a company or organization, but who provides services as needed; they do not receive a regular salary or fringe benefits, but are paid by the hour or project

hacker: the term for both people who seek to use their computer and hacking skills to do good, and those who use their talents to do bad

literature classes: those that provide more information on and analysis of the best novels, non-fiction, poetry, plays, and other works of writing by authors from around the world

Chapter 3

PREPARING FOR THE FIELD AND MAKING A LIVING

EDUCATIONAL PATHS

You can train to become a computer game or app developer via several methods. Many developers have bachelor's degrees in technology- and design-related fields. Some people receive training via a short apprenticeship or through the military. A degree or other formal training is not absolutely necessary to become a game or app developer. Some developers are creative and technical whizzes and began creating and selling games or apps while they were in college, or even high school. But this entry path is becoming rare because employers want applicants who have completed at least some post–high school training. The following sections provide more information on educational preparation.

High school students work on a project during computer science class.

HIGH SCHOOL CLASSES

As a teenager, you've probably been using apps and playing video games ever since you were a toddler. As a result, it's almost certain that you're terrific with technology. But regardless of your skill level, there are many technical and non-technical classes that you can take in high school that will prepare you for college or other training programs.

You don't have to have a high IQ to know that you should take computer science classes. Some recommended courses include:

- Introduction to Computer Science

- Computer Programming

- Software Development

- Introduction to Game Design

- Computer Security

Art and design classes (especially those in digital art and 2-D and 3-D modeling) will help you to develop your creativity and artistic skills. In these courses, you'll learn what it takes to turn a burst of creative inspiration into a finished work of art—whether it's a painting or sculpture, or digital art you create using design software.

Although the video games and app development industries are very creative, it's still necessary to have detailed rules and guidelines that dictate what can happen from screen to screen, what characters can and can't do in every situation, and countless other game playing or app use scenarios. Mathematical concepts provide the technical framework behind these rules, especially pertaining to 3-D modeling and software programming. Take the following classes to build your math skills:

- algebra

- trigonometry

- calculus

- linear algebra

- discrete mathematics

- applied mathematics

Game and app developers who write scripts need excellent writing skills. To develop your writing talents, take **literature classes**, as well as composition and creative writing courses. Additionally, speech classes will help you to develop your oral communication skills. You'll need these to communicate effectively with members of your team and give presentations about your work.

Other useful high school classes include:

- social studies

- physics

- history

- foreign language

- business, marketing, and accounting (if you plan to start a company)

Learn how students are earning money for college by participating in e-sports competitions

TYPES OF EDUCATION CREDENTIALS

A **certificate** shows that a person has completed specialized education, passed a test, and met other requirements to qualify for work in a career or industry. College certificate programs typically last six months to a year.

A student earns an **associate's degree** after they complete two years of post-high school education at a community or technical college.

A student earns a **bachelor's degree** in one of two ways:

- by earning an associate's degree and completing two additional years of education at a four-year college or university

- by graduating from high school and completing four years of education at a four-year college or university.

A **master's degree** is a graduate-level credential that is awarded to a student after they first complete a four-year bachelor's degree, then complete two additional years of education.

A student earns a **doctoral degree** after first earning a bachelor's and master's degree. To earn a doctorate (also known as a PhD), students must conduct original research, prepare a dissertation (a type of long report), and defend their dissertation before a committee of professors.

COLLEGES AND UNIVERSITIES

Many developers have bachelor's degrees in software design, computer programming, game development, computer science, digital design, digital art and animation, multimedia arts, or related areas. Others earn certificates or associate's degrees in these fields.

To be eligible for managerial and executive positions at large computer companies, you'll need a master's degree in a computer- or design-related field, or a degree in project management or business management. If you decide to teach game development, computer science, or another subject at a college or university, you'll need to have at least a master's degree, but preferably a doctoral degree.

In the United States, more than 520 colleges and universities offer degrees in game design or in related specialties. The Entertainment Software Association offers a list of these programs at www.theesa.com/about-esa/courses-certificates-degree-programs. In 1994, DigiPen Institute of Technology became the first school in North America to offer a two-year degree in video game programming. Today, the institute offers associate and bachelor's degrees in a variety of game-related areas. Students in its Game Design program focus on the following subjects:

- Game design and development, including game mechanics and history, design documentation, scripting and programming, 2-D and 3-D level design, character design, playtesting, interface design, product management, and team game project implementation

An apprentice (second from right) receives instruction from a team of app developers.

- Humanities and arts, including writing, psychology, film, audio, architecture, drawing, and 2-D and 3-D art, with the option to study advanced topics in these areas

- Foundational math and science courses, including the fundamentals of scripting languages, mathematics, and physics

College students typically complete at least one internship as part of their training. An internship is a paid or unpaid learning opportunity in which a student works at a business to get experience. It can last anywhere from a few weeks to a year. Your college's career services office can help you find internships in game or app design. You can also visit the websites of game and app design companies to see if they offer formal internship programs.

Internships are occasionally available to high school students and young adults who are interested in changing careers.

THE BEST VIDEO GAME DESIGN PROGRAMS

Each year, The Princeton Review surveys colleges and universities to identify the top fifty video game design programs in the United States and Canada. Schools are assessed based on their game design academic offerings, lab facilities, and the starting salaries and career achievements of graduates. Here were the top fifteen undergraduate programs in 2018. Visit www.princetonreview.com/college-rankings/game-design for the complete list.

1. University of Southern California (Los Angeles, CA)
2. New York University (Brooklyn, NY)
3. DigiPen Institute of Technology (Redmond, WA)
4. Becker College (Worcester, MA)
5. Rochester Institute of Technology (Rochester, NY)
6. University of Utah (Salt Lake City, UT)
7. Michigan State University (East Lansing, MI)
8. Worcester Polytechnic Institute (Worcester, MA)
9. Hampshire College (Amherst, MA)
10. LaSalle College Vancouver (Vancouver, BC)
11. Drexel University (Philadelphia, PA)
12. Champlain College (Burlington, VT)
13. Cogswell College (San Jose, CA)
14. Vancouver Film School (Vancouver, BC)
15. Bradley University (Peoria, IL)

APPRENTICESHIPS

When most people think of apprenticeships, they think of a plumbing apprentice learning how to fix a leaky pipe or a carpentry apprentice being trained to build framing at a construction site. But did you know that apprenticeships are available in hundreds of careers—even game design? Apprenticeships have become more popular in a wider range of fields because company executives have realized that they're an excellent way to identify and train future employees.

Game development apprenticeships typically last from twelve weeks to a year—a much shorter training period than what is required for trade apprenticeships. Participating in an apprenticeship is a great way to prepare for a career because, unlike college, you do not have to pay tuition and you do receive a salary.

Game development apprenticeships are available to college students and recent college graduates. Eligibility requirements include experience developing web and/or mobile applications or computer games via collegiate education, attending a coding or design **bootcamp**, or focusing on self-guided learning; using popular game and/or app development software; excellent communication skills; the ability to work well under deadline pressure; a team-oriented mindset; and an interest in learning new things.

Opportunities can be found by contacting game and app development companies or by conducting a keyword search on the internet using phrases such as "game design apprenticeships."

MILITARY

When you think of the military, images of real guns, tanks, jeeps, and fighter jets probably race through your mind—not fun video games or helpful apps. But the various branches of the U.S. military (Air Force, Army, Coast Guard, Marines, and Navy) use technology in almost every aspect of their operations. They need computer experts to manage information technology systems, developers and programmers to write and troubleshoot code, information security analysts to protect computers from **hackers**, and many other types of technology professionals.

One potential training path is in computer programming. Trainees learn how to:

- Use current programming languages

- Plan, design, and test computer systems

- Write code to develop software programs

- Debug software

- Protect computers from hackers

While you train, you'll receive a salary and will not have to pay any tuition, but you will have to make a service commitment of two to four years. Ask your recruiter for more information.

The U.S. military offers training in other computer-related careers that can be a starting point for entering the game and app design fields, including software developer, network and computer systems administrator, information security analyst, and multimedia artist/animator. You can learn more about these and other careers at Today'sMilitary.com. Militaries in other countries also provide computer training.

THE LARGEST GAME MARKETS IN THE WORLD

1. China

2. United States

3. Japan

4. South Korea

5. Germany

6. United Kingdom

Source: Newzoo

GETTING A JOB

"I have to get a job!?," you ask in astonishment. Yes, it's true. You will eventually need to get a full-time job to pay for the housing, food, and fun activities that your parents currently take care of. But the good news (unless you're really excited about going to work) is that you don't have to start right now while you're still in school. But it's never too early to learn how the job search process works. After all, the more you know about networking, accessing resources from professional associations, and using job boards and other job search tools, the better off you'll be when it comes time to look for your first job. You can also use these resources to help find an internship while you're in college or even high school. Here are some popular job search methods for job hunters.

USE YOUR NETWORK

A computer network is a collection of interconnected computers that communicate with each other and perform tasks. But did you know that there is another type of network that is helpful to computer professionals and anyone who is looking for a job or internship, or wants to achieve other life goals?

Networking simply involves talking with people you know, making new friends, exchanging information, and assisting others when they need help.

It might come as a surprise that you already have a network! Your personal network consists of your friends, classmates, and family, friends. You use this type of network when you need answers to such questions as: "I missed class! What's going to be on the quiz tomorrow?", "When's football practice?", or "Do you know any business that needs summer workers?"

EMPLOYERS OF COMPUTER GAME AND APP DEVELOPERS

- Computer game and app development companies

- Nonprofit organizations

- Colleges and universities

- Government agencies

- Military

- Any company or organization that wants to create a computer game or app

Once you get to college or pursue another type of post–high school training, you'll also become part of a professional network that includes your teachers, internship or apprenticeship directors, coaches, classmates, bosses, and people you meet online, including at social networking sites such as LinkedIn.

Be sure to take networking seriously and begin developing your network as soon as possible. It's an important tool that will help you to learn more about potential employers, make new connections that can help you get a job, and obtain all types of information that is useful regardless of where you're at in life (i.e., high school student, apprentice, college student, or game or app developer).

Your fellow interns can be great networking resources.

BUILDING A PORTFOLIO

A portfolio consists of your best design and/or programming work. Job applicants use their portfolio to demonstrate their abilities to hiring managers. Having a portfolio is especially important in creative fields, such as game and app development, because employers don't just want to read about the classes you took or the degree you completed. They want to see that you can code, debug in several different programming languages, or develop games or apps in various areas. If you're still training for the field, you can include school/apprenticeship projects, as well as your best personal projects, in your portfolio. Visit www.gamedesigning.org/career/game-design-portfolio to learn how to create a game design portfolio.

CHECK OUT JOB BOARDS

Many professional associations, businesses, and other organizations have internet job boards that list internships and job openings. While you're probably a few years from applying for an internship or job, it's a good idea to check out some job listings to see what types of education and skills are in demand. Here are a few game and app development job boards:

- https://careers.igda.org

- www.gamejobs.com

- www.gamasutra.com

- https://dribbble.com/jobs

And here are some general job sites that offer game and app development job listings:

- www.indeed.com

- www.linkedin.com

- www.dice.com

- www.cybercareers.gov/job-seeker (U.S. government job board)

- www.jobbank.gc.ca (Canadian government job board)

- www.gov.uk/jobsearch (United Kingdom government job board)

JOIN AND USE THE RESOURCES OF PROFESSIONAL ASSOCIATIONS

A professional association is an organization that is founded by a group of people who have the same career (game developers, professional hackers, biologists, etc.) or who work in the same industry specialty (information technology, hospitality, etc.). These organizations offer a wealth of career exploration and job search resources for aspiring computer game and app developers. They provide membership (including categories for students), training opportunities, job listings, discussion boards, networking events, and much more.

If you're looking for a job—or just want to learn more about a career or industry—association websites should be some of your first stops. Here are some major professional associations for computer game and app developers around the world.

- Academy of Interactive Arts & Sciences: www.interactive.org

- Entertainment Software Association: www.theesa.com

- Game Developers' Association of Australia: www.gdaa.com.au

- International Game Developers Association: www.igda.org

- Irish Game Makers Association: www.imirt.ie

- UK Interactive Entertainment Association: https://ukie.org.uk

SALARIES FOR MULTIMEDIA ARTISTS AND ANIMATORS BY U.S. STATE

Multimedia artists and animators work in the fields of game design, as well as film and television animation. They earn a wide range of salaries based on their training, job duties, where they work, and other factors. Here are the five states where employers pay the highest average salary and the states in which employers pay the lowest salaries.

Highest Average Salaries:

1. Connecticut: $91,940

2. Washington: $88,240

3. California: $85,340

4. New York: $79,720

5. Oregon: $77,450

Source: U.S. Department of Labor

Lowest Average Salaries:

1. South Dakota: $39,360

2. South Carolina: $39,430

3. Montana: $42,190

4. Indiana: $45,030

5. Nebraska: $48,280

HOW MUCH CAN I EARN?

Earnings for computer game and app developers vary by job title, educational background, their level of experience, whether they work full or part time, and other factors. For example, an app developer at a large company will make more money than someone who works at a small "mom and pop" firm. An experienced app developer who has a long track record of creating best-selling apps will earn much more than the average developer just out of college.

The median annual salary for multimedia artists and animators (who work in the fields of game design and film and television animation) is $70,530, according to the U.S. Department of Labor (USDL). The lowest paid professionals earn less than $39,330 per year, and the highest earners receive $123,060 or more per year.

Salaries for software application designers range from less than $59,870 to $160,100 or more, according to the USDL. They earn median annual salaries of $101,790.

Lead application developers earned salaries that ranged from $104,000 to $178,000, according to Robert Half Technology's *Salary Guide for Technology Professionals*. Salaries for mobile application developers ranged from $119,500 to $204,250.

Computer game and app developers who work full time (35–40 hours a week) for companies and other organizations often receive fringe benefits such as health insurance, paid vacation and sick days, and other perks. **Freelancers** do not receive these benefits.

Software developers earn salaries that are significantly higher than those received by people in many other careers.

TEXT-DEPENDENT QUESTIONS:

1. What high school classes should you take to prepare for a career in game development?
2. What are the two types of networks?
3. What type of developers earn the highest salaries?

RESEARCH PROJECT:

Interview game and app developers who trained for the field via college, an apprenticeship, and the military. Ask them what they liked and disliked about this training method and what they would do differently if they could repeat their training. Create a chart that lists the pros and cons of each educational approach. Which is the best approach for you? Write a 250-word report that explains why you think this form of training is the best option

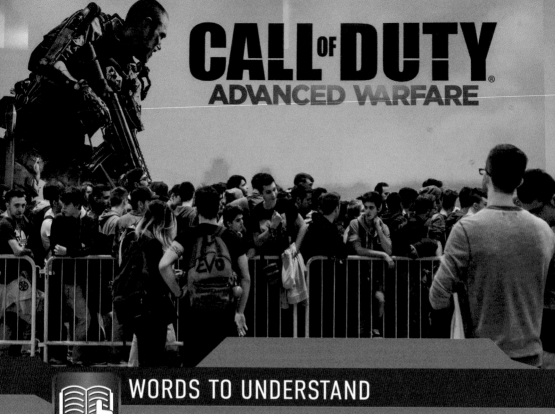

WORDS TO UNDERSTAND

capstone: in academia, a final class that seeks to summarize all that a student has learned in a program

constructive criticism: assessments from one's friends, family, and coworkers that are not meant to be negative, but aim to help an individual improve their performance

dialogue: what characters say to one another in a video game, television show, film, or play

market research: the process of gathering information to learn more about potential and existing customers

promotion: receiving a higher-level job

Chapter 4

KEY SKILLS AND METHODS OF EXPLORATION

SKILL BUILDING LEADS TO SUCCESS

Computer game and app developers need technical skills (knowledge of programming languages, game engines, etc.), but they also need soft skills. These skills—such as the ability to communicate effectively, solve problems, and work as a member of a team—are the traits that will make you stand out from other job applicants and coworkers (once you get hired). Having good soft skills gets you the job, helps you to do your work better, and makes you qualified for a **promotion** and a pay raise. Here are some key traits for developers.

IMAGINATION AND CREATIVITY

Game and app developers are creative people with great imaginations. They are able to create a finished product (e.g., a role-playing adventure game, a business networking app, etc.) from an idea in their head. They are inspired by the world around them—

To be successful in this career, you'll need strong interpersonal and communication skills.

everything from nature to the cool way someone is dressed in a coffee shop to the futuristic design of a skyscraper they see on their way to work. They are always generating ideas to try out in their games and apps. Creativity also comes in handy when a developer needs to solve the inevitable problems that arise during development.

COMMUNICATION AND INTERPERSONAL SKILLS

During the course of a project, you'll interact with people with all knowledge ranges and backgrounds, from fellow designers, writers, and artists who know tech and design lingo to company executives who don't. In some positions, you may even conduct **market research** with potential users—young people, the elderly, or others—so you should be comfortable interacting with others.

DETAIL-ORIENTED

Details are crucial in game and app development. Hundreds, if not thousands, of steps are required to create a mass-market app or video game, so developers must be extremely detail-oriented and focused as they do their work. If you lack this skill, you will encounter major challenges on the job. For example, if you rush through writing character **dialogue**, it may sound stilted and unbelievable. If you fail to test your game on different systems, it may not work for some of your customers. Finally, if you forget to back up your work (two million lines of C++ code in thirty-five modules, for example), a hard drive crash could turn your dream game into a nightmare.

PASSION

Employers don't want employees who just do their jobs. They want workers who love their jobs, who are obsessed with video games or apps, who geek out when they create a cool video game character or fight scene, and who live and dream video games or app development. Developers who are passionate about their work get noticed, get the good assignments, and get promoted.

SELF-MOTIVATED

Every game or app development project will have a clear set of goals and a firm deadline, but that's often where the rules stop. In many positions, it will be up to you to determine how to get the job done, frequently without the oversight of a manager. You'll need to be able to effectively manage your time, push yourself to keep going when you get tired or frustrated, be accountable to yourself and to others, and do whatever it takes to get the job done correctly on time.

PROBLEM-SOLVING SKILLS

With their complex combination of design, plot, dialogue, audio, animation, programming code, and other components, it should come as no surprise that problems will arise as you develop games and apps. For example, game characters may not appear as lifelike as you wanted, some functions of an app may not work as planned, or bugs may arise when a tester navigates through a specific fight sequence. When a problem occurs, you'll be on the spot to fix it. Good problem solvers are creative and analytical thinkers, are patient, and have the tenacity to keep trying different solutions until the issue is addressed.

HUMILITY

You may think your idea for a new computer game is the greatest thing since *Fortnite*. You may believe that you're the most creative person in the world, or that you're the best software developer since Bjarne Stroustrup (the creator of the programming language C++, which is a key tool in game development). It's easy to get cocky in the game and app business, but you need to be humble and face reality. You may be talented, but there are many creative whizzes in the industry. Your first ideas for a new game may not be

A developer can't contain her enthusiasm as she uses virtual reality goggles to test a game.

as amazing as you think they are—and your teammates will let you know if that's the case. Game developers typically have no problem telling others what they think. As a result, you need to not get overconfident, be respectful with your colleagues, and learn to accept **constructive criticism**.

BUSINESS SKILLS

Some game and app developers are not just happy working for others. They decide to start a business. If you decide to become an entrepreneur, you'll quickly need to become an expert in basic accounting, marketing, bidding on jobs, social media, managing staff, and doing other tasks that keep your company running smoothly. Something to keep in mind: just because you're good at programming and designing games or apps doesn't mean that you're going to be good at business. If you decide to launch a company, take the time to learn the aforementioned skills so that your company is the business equivalent of *Minecraft*, not *Bubsy 3D*, which is frequently included on "Worst Video Games of All Time" lists.

DAY IN THE LIFE: GAME TESTER

When people ask me what I do, I love telling them I'm a "bug hunter." Some people think I'm an exterminator, while others quickly get what I really do—I search for bugs and other issues on computer games.

I don't plan to be a bug hunter forever. It's just my strategy to break into the computer gaming industry. That's how many of the top developers got started in the field. It's a good fit for me because you don't need a computer science degree to get hired (I'm still in college and do this work part time), and my position allows me to get a close-up look at every aspect of game development.

When I'm gametesting, I look for all types of issues. For example, dead ends are places in a game (often in action adventure, first-person shooter, and real-time strategy games) where the player can no longer progress because of a programming glitch. Then there's quality of gameplay issues such as "spawn camping," in which the game is designed so that a player in a shooter game may be allowed to "camp out" in the spot where his enemy reproduces to kill them as they come to life. Although spawn camping is not technically breaking the rules, it's extremely frustrating to the opponent of a spawn camper, so I write a note to the developer that describes the situation.

When I playtest, I pretend that I'm just a regular player. So if spawn camping irritates me, it will probably irritate other users. In this situation, the developer might revise the game scenario so that the spawn has a shield or it can hatch in a protected area. I also identify loopholes, in which a player discovers an unplanned advantage inadvertently created by the developer that allows them to win the game or acquire wealth, fighting skills, weapons, etc., that give them a big competitive advantage. We also may be asked to focus on what a certain character can do or not do in a game, so I follow that character throughout the game—testing, testing, and testing as I go.

Other times, we're asked to do something as monotonous as running into every castle wall (in a game with twenty levels!) to make sure that they're all solid. As I playtest, I have to write up bug reports and use specialized software such as JIRA or Bugzilla to explain what happened and how it happened (what I was doing when the problem occurred).

This work can be monotonous at times and the pay is pretty low, but I still enjoy finding bugs and other issues. If you love video games and enjoy solving puzzles, working as a game tester is a good entry-level way to break into the gaming industry.

EXPLORING GAME AND APP DESIGN AS A STUDENT

There are many ways to learn more about computer game and app design and careers in the field. An easy way to gain experience is to play as many games and try out as many apps as possible. Here are some other popular methods of exploration.

JOIN THE TECHNOLOGY STUDENT ASSOCIATION (TSA)

If you're a middle school or high school student and interested in science, technology, engineering, and mathematics, consider joining the TSA (www.tsaweb.org). This national nonprofit organization offers sixty competitions at its annual conference—including those

A teen plays *Fortnite*, a popular online multiplayer video game.

Taking game design classes is an excellent way to build your skills.

in video game design, coding, software development, system control technology, and technology problem-solving. (A nonprofit organization is a group that uses any profits it generates to advance its stated goals. It is not a corporation or other for-profit business.) The TSA also provides opportunities to develop your leadership skills and compete for money for college. Ask your school counselor or science teacher if your school has a TSA chapter and, if not, ask them to start one.

TAKE A CLASS

If you're interested in game and app development, you're going to take plenty of technology-related classes in high school and college, but did you know that private organizations, professional associations, and other organizations also provide these courses, both in person and online? These classes are a good way to develop your skills and see if a career in game or app development is in your future. One great example is Coursera.org, which offers a Game Design and Development Specialization that features five classes:

- Introduction to Game Development
- Principles of Game Design
- Business of Games and Entrepreneurship
- Game Development for Modern Platforms
- Game Design and Development **Capstone**

ATTEND A SUMMER CAMP

Summer game design, programming, and general computer science camps and workshops are offered by colleges and universities, high schools, community groups, museums, private tech organizations, and other groups.

Some camps charge a program fee, while others are free. Camps that charge a program fee sometimes give scholarships to campers to reduce the cost of attendance. There are two types of camps: day and residential. At a day camp, you go home after each session. At a residential camp, you stay overnight in college dormitories or other comfortable buildings.

Ask your computer science teacher or school counselor for help finding summer camps and workshops. Here are several examples of well-known camps in the United States and Canada. Camps are also available in other countries.

NATIONAL STUDENT LEADERSHIP CONFERENCE ON GAME DESIGN

This organization offers a nine-day summer game design program for high school students that is held two times each summer at the University of Washington in the United States. If you participate in this program, you'll learn about 3-D characters, animation, sound effects, and the mechanics of game creation, including scripting, level development, programming, sound effects, and lighting. You'll even create a new video or mobile game. And you'll get a chance to talk with a variety of professionals, including game designers, programmers, and testers. The program is residential and requires a fee, but scholarships are available. Learn more at www.nslcleaders.org/youth-leadership-programs/game-design.

IDTECH

Each year, iDTech (www.idtech.com) hosts more than 60,000 residential campers ages seven to nineteen at 150 colleges and universities in the United States, the United Kingdom, South Korea, Taiwan, Hong Kong, and Singapore. It offers camp paths in Game Development, Coding, Robotics, and Design. These are fee-based camps. Some recent camps included:

- Game Design and Development 101
- Code Cafe: Make Games with Java
- Code Apps with C++
- Develop and Code Games with C++
- *Fortnite* Camp and Unreal Engine Level Design
- Twitch Game Streaming and Video Production

DIGITAL MEDIA ACADEMY

The academy offers one- and two-week Game Design Camps for young people ages twelve to seventeen at locations throughout the United States and Canada. In these camps, you'll learn game design processes, how to create clear and efficient code, how to troubleshoot errors and solve logic problems, and much more. The academy is sponsored by the

Stanford University Continuing Studies Department. Learn more at www.digitalmediaacademy.org/game-design-development-camps.

FINDING MORE CAMPS

Many other colleges, organizations, and businesses offer summer game development, programming, and general computer science camps. Contact schools and organizations in your area to learn more.

E-SPORTS: GAMING FOR FUN AND PRIZES

E-sports is a term that is used to describe organized competitive video gaming events in which people of all ages compete against one another live for the chance to win cash prizes. Top players can earn more than $1 million a year.

This form of competitive gaming is not just popular among the players. Approximately 380 million people worldwide watched e-sports in 2018, according to a report from Newzoo, a market analytics company. Fans can watch e-sports competitions by attending live events or by tuning in on TV, or online through streaming services such as Twitch.

E-sports have become very popular on college campuses. More than fifty colleges and universities have varsity e-sports programs that are recognized by the National Association of Collegiate Esports.

Annual revenue in the e-sports industry grew from $194 million in 2014 to $463 million in 2016, according to Newzoo. It's expected to surpass $1 billion annually in the next year or so.

An event at the Counter-Strike: Global Offensive e-sports tournament.

PARTICIPATE IN A COMPETITION

Gaming associations, tech companies, schools, and other organizations sponsor contests that allow you to match your skills and knowledge with others who are interested in game and app development. The winners of some competitions get cash prizes or college scholarship money. Others just get bragging rights. Winners also might get noticed by potential employers. Check out the following competitions:

SkillsUSA

SkillsUSA is a national membership organization for middle school, high school, and college students who are preparing for careers in technical, trade, and skilled service occupations. It offers several competitions for those who are interested in computers and other technology. Competitions include Interactive Application and Video Game Design, Computer Programming, Technical Computer Applications, and Web Design. SkillsUSA works directly with high schools and colleges, so ask your school counselor or teacher if it is an option for you. Learn more at www.skillsusa.org.

SKILLS COMPÉTENCES CANADA

Skills Compétences Canada is a nonprofit organization that seeks to encourage Canadian youth to pursue careers in the skilled technology and trades sectors. Its National Competition allows young people to participate in more than forty skilled trade and technology competitions. In its 3-D Character Computer Animation competition, contestants are provided with a sound clip and are given twelve hours to develop storyboards, animatics, and animations based on the sound clip. A 2-D Character Computer Animation competition is also available. Learn more at www. skillscompetencescanada.com/en/skills-canada-national-competition.

SOURCES OF ADDITIONAL EXPLORATION

Contact the following organizations for more information on education and careers in the game and app development industry, certification, and membership:

Academy of Interactive Arts & Sciences
www.interactive.org

Association for Computing Machinery
www.acm.org

Entertainment Software Association
www.theesa.com

Game Developers' Association of Australia
www.gdaa.com.au

IEEE Computer Society
www.computer.org

International Game Developers Association
www.igda.org

Irish Game Makers Association
www.imirt.ie

UK Interactive Entertainment Association
https://ukie.org.uk

BECOME A SCOUT

The Boy Scouts and Girl Scouts are membership organizations for those ages roughly five to eighteen (age ranges vary by country and group). If you join one of these organizations, you'll learn how to become a better citizen and person. You also learn about a variety of topics—from camping and pet care, to law and information technology. When you learn something new in scouts, you usually receive a merit badge or other type of award.

If you are a boy or a girl in the United States, you can join the Boy Scouts of America (www.scouting.org) and earn a merit badge in Game Design. To qualify for this badge, you must demonstrate your knowledge of the types of games and design basics, create a design proposal for a new game, talk with game developers, and meet other criteria. Additionally, merit badges are available in Animation, Digital Technology, and Programming. Members of the Girl Scouts of the United States of America (www.girlscouts.org) can earn merit badges in Programming, Entertainment Technology, and other fields.

You don't have to live in the United States to be a scout. Scouts Australia (https://scouts.com.au), which was founded in 1908, has approximately 70,000 members. Scouting organizations in Great Britain include The Scout Association (https://scouts.org.uk) and British Boy Scouts and British Girl Scouts Association (https://bbsandbgs.org.uk). If you live in Canada, you can join Scouts Canada (www.scouts.ca).

OTHER WAYS TO LEARN MORE ABOUT GAME AND APP DEVELOPMENT

- Attend video game and development conferences

- Read books and watch videos about game and app development

- Visit the websites of college and university game and app development programs

- Talk to your school counselor about career opportunities in game and app development

- Work with your school counselor or computer science teacher to organize a tech career fair

CONDUCT AN INFORMATION INTERVIEW

An information interview simply involves talking to a developer about their career. You can conduct this interview in person at the developer's work site, on the telephone, via email, or through video-conferencing software online. Here are some questions to ask during the interview:

- Can you tell me about a day in your life on the job?

- What are the most important personal and professional qualities for developers?

- What do you like best and least about your job?

- Is your job stressful? If so, please explain why.

- What is the future employment outlook for developers? How is the field changing?

- How did you prepare for this career?

- What can I do now to prepare for the field?

Visitors test their gaming skills at a video game conference.

TEXT-DEPENDENT QUESTIONS:

1. Why is it important for developers to be creative?

2. What can you learn at a game development summer camp?

3. What is information interviewing?

RESEARCH PROJECT:

Conduct interviews with developers at different companies. Ask them questions from the list in the information interviewing section. Write a report that compares and contrasts the job duties and educational requirements for each worker.

 ## WORDS TO UNDERSTAND

cloud computing: computer services that are provided over the internet instead of on a personal computer or local server; sometimes referred to as *the cloud*

denigrate: to unfairly criticize someone

discrimination: treating people badly because of their race, religion, gender, age, or other factors

lucrative: a business or investment that makes a lot of money

proficient: skilled at something

revenue: money earned from the sales of goods or services

Chapter 5

THE FUTURE OF COMPUTER GAME AND APP DEVELOPMENT

THE BIG PICTURE

The employment outlook in computer game and app development is expected to be good during the next decade. Employment for software developers (who are sometimes known as *software engineers*) is projected to increase by 24 percent from 2016 to 2026, according to the U.S. Department of Labor (USDL). This is much faster than the average for all careers. The USDL says that "prospects will be best for applicants with knowledge of the most up-to-date programming tools and for those who are **proficient** in one or more programming languages." Additionally, the information technology staffing firm Robert Half Technology included the career of developer on its list of "In-Demand Technology Roles."

Job opportunities for multimedia artists and animators are projected to increase by 8 percent from 2016 to 2026, or about as fast as the average for all occupations. Projected growth will occur because of increased demand for animation and visual effects in video games, movies, and television. "Consumers will continue to demand more realistic video games, movie, and television special effects, and three-dimensional movies," according to the USDL. It also predicts than an increased need for computer graphics for mobile devices, such as smartphones, will lead to more job opportunities.

Opportunities for software developers will also be strong outside the United States, according to the recruitment firm Michael Page. It reports that there is a shortage of software developers in Australia, Belgium, Brazil, Canada, Chile, Czech Republic, Denmark, Estonia, France, Germany, Greece, Ireland, Israel, Japan, Korea, Luxembourg, Mexico, Netherlands, New Zealand, Russia, Slovak Republic, Sweden, and the United Kingdom.

The shortage of some information technology workers is so severe in New Zealand that the country added the careers of software engineer, software tester, developer programmer, and software and applications programmer to its Immigration New Zealand long-term skill shortage list. The list serves as an advertisement to workers from other countries to encourage them to come to New Zealand to work.

In the United Kingdom (U.K.), the video game industry generates more **revenue** than the video or music industries. There are more than 2,175 game development firms in the U.K., according to Gamesmap.uk.

DAY IN THE LIFE: APP DEVELOPER

I've worked in app development for fifteen years. I'm probably best known for helping to launch a relatively well-known microblogging and social networking site. I was not the public face of this four-person startup. I liked geeking out on the backend programming: making the servers work, doing database stuff, making things go faster, and deleting old code that was unnecessary. I won't mention the name of this company because I've left it, I'm not happy with its current direction, and I still have good friends there. But I've moved on to some great new opportunities.

Your job duties as an app developer will vary based on where you work. For example, when I worked at the microblogging and social networking startup, we simply tackled the most pressing task and just kept working down our list until we would temporarily catch up. The lifestyle was hectic and draining. There were a lot of late nights, long weekends, stressful team meetings, and fast-food lunches and dinners. Now that I'm older, I would not want to keep up that pace again.

Now I'm the CEO of an app development startup. I spend 25 to 30 percent of my time trying to get funding from investors and maybe 30 percent doing design work. I spend the remaining 40 to 45 percent of my day managing the developers, helping out (creating wireframes, writing code, app testing, and doing other tasks), and generally keeping things on track. Running an app development company is like captaining a ship, in a way. If you don't keep your ship sailing well, it gets a little off course every day. At first, it may not be noticeable, but within a short time, you're way off course and headed for an iceberg!

It might sound cliché, but my favorite part of the job is seeing people actually using my apps and getting benefits from them.

If you're thinking about becoming an app developer, just do it. Jump right in in whatever capacity you can—app testing, marketing, etc. Get your foot in the door, keep learning, and if you're talented, you'll move into a development position.

Another thing: Don't get a big head. Be honest with yourself. Even though I've made a good living, some of my ideas are just terrible! If you own a company, build a good team around you that's willing to tell you what they really think. It makes a difference. Finally, consider specializing in developing apps for Android. Even though I find Android kind of annoying at times, demand is higher in this specialty because no one wants to do it!

CHALLENGES TO EMPLOYMENT GROWTH

Demand for computer game and app developers is good in many countries, but there a few trends that could slow employment growth. As game and app development becomes more automated (with the help of artificial intelligence—

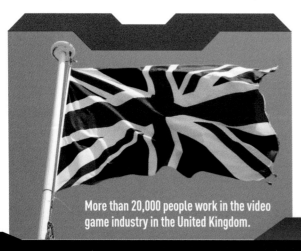

More than 20,000 people work in the video game industry in the United Kingdom.

AI, the simulation of human intelligence by machinery and computer systems), demand may decline for developers. But there is such a wide variety of games and apps (and new uses being developed for these products every day) that developers should not expect to be replaced by AI anytime soon. While it's true that AI-powered computers will take over some low-level tasks—such as basic coding and testing—developers will still be needed to use their creativity, advanced development skills, and other skills to create computer games and apps.

Employment opportunities in computer game and app development may decline in developed countries such as the United States, Canada, and Germany if companies choose to hire developers who work in less-developed countries where these employees receive lower salaries. Developers who become skilled in the latest programming languages and knowledgeable about game and app development trends (virtual reality, augmented reality, AI, etc.) have the best chances of staying employed.

Demand will continue to be strong for app developers during the next decade.

Finally, there may be fewer job openings for developers if more people enter this career. Many young people want to enter these careers because they're exciting, rewarding, fun, and **lucrative**. If this occurs, you may need to move to another city to land a job or go back to school (or take online classes) to learn the latest programming languages. Keep in mind that talented and skilled developers always can get a job. You just need to keep your skills up to date and continue to do the best work that you can. If you do this, you'll find a job in the computer game or app development industries.

WOMEN IN GAME DEVELOPMENT

Although 41 percent of women are computer game players, only about 21 percent of developers are female. There are several reasons why more women aren't pursuing careers in game development, including high levels of **discrimination** and sexual harassment, lack of advancement opportunities, and lower earnings than men. The gaming industry is attempting to increase the number of women entering this field by taking a close look at how their games sometimes **denigrate** women, establishing zero-tolerance policies regarding discrimination and sexual harassment, hosting open houses at high school and colleges to educate young women about opportunities in the gaming industry, founding support groups, and establishing mentorship programs. Here are a few organizations that support women in game development and other computer fields:

Sources: Entertainment Software Association, Statista.com

- Women in Games: www.womeningames.org

- International Game Developers Association Women in Games Special Interest Group: https://women.igda.org

- Women in Development, Games & Everything Tech: www.widgetau.com

- Association for Women in Computing: www.awc-hq.org

- IEEE Computer Society-Women in Computing: www.computer.org/web/communities/women-in-computing

- National Center for Women & Information Technology: www.ncwit.org

There are many opportunities for women in game development and e-sports.

The jury is still out on whether virtual reality will become the main component in computer games, or just a supporting technology.

THE FUTURE OF COMPUTER GAMES AND APPS

The computer game industry has changed significantly since the first computer game, *Spacewar*, was created in 1962 by a college student. *Spacewar* was a simple space game that featured two spaceships battling it out on a black screen with some white stars in the background. (You can view this game on YouTube.com.) Today, games are highly complex and visually stunning. Some are considered almost works of art. Additionally, a lot has changed in the app industry since the first mobile app appeared on the Nokia 9000 Communicator (what we now call a smartphone) in 1996. Today, apps are everywhere, and they are immensely more user-friendly and powerful than those that were produced even ten years ago. So what does the future hold for computer game and app development? Here are a few things that may occur.

- Augmented reality (AR), a computer-generated system that combines a virtual environment with imaginary elements that are introduced to a real environment, will continue to be integrated into games and apps. The majority of AR game play may move from smartphones to AR glasses and headsets.

- Virtual reality (VR), a computer-generated experience that takes place within a simulated environment using headgear or other equipment that shuts out the real world, will continue to be integrated into games and apps, but developers disagree on its importance to the gaming industry. Some developers believe that VR gaming will become the dominant game platform. Others are not convinced. "VR doesn't make sense—or add much—to many game genres," explained Nick Yee, head of game analytics consultancy Quantic Foundry, in an interview about the trend at Polygon.com, a gaming website. "And because the appeal of being immersed in an alternate world isn't the primary gaming motivation for many gamers, these gamers would be unlikely to invest in expensive VR equipment." Given the diversity of opinions, aspiring and current developers will just have to stay tuned to determine what role VR will play in future games.

- The computer game and app development industries will continue to become more welcoming to women and ethnic minorities as companies realize that these groups make up a large number of game and app users. As a result, the development process will benefit as developers from more diverse backgrounds are able to contribute their ideas. Just as the blockbuster movie *Black Panther* helped to bust movie studio stereotypes regarding minority-directed and -acted movies, the emergence of women and minority developers in the game and app development industries will have the same effect.

- Video games will increasingly be used not to just provide fun, but to also educate people about a wide range of topics.

- More video games will be offered via **cloud computing** as advances in technology make it easier to play online and internet connections become faster and more reliable. Cloud-based games are streamed via a high-speed internet connection to the player on a computer, television, or other supported device. Gamers are embracing cloud-based video games because their use eliminates the need to buy an expensive game console or a hard copy of the actual game. Game companies like this approach because it guarantees a steady revenue stream from subscriptions.

- Many current computer games are designed for people who are under the age of fifty. As the average age of people in the United States and other nations continues to rise, more games will be created for older players. More intergenerational games, which are appealing to both young and old, will also be developed.

- Free game- and app-making tools such as Unity and GameMaker will allow more people to become developers. Although this is a positive step overall, the availability of free or low-cost game or app development software will greatly increase the number of games and apps being produced. This may make it harder to get a job in the field and to get one's game or app noticed in the marketplace.

Eleven developers offer their predictions on the future of gaming

IN CONCLUSION

Do you love playing computer games or using apps? Are you creative and have a great imagination? Do you have great technical skills and enjoy solving problems? Are you looking for a career that offers good pay, the chance to use your creativity every day, and great job prospects? If so, then a career as a computer game or app developer could be in your future.

I hope that you'll use this book as a starting point to discover even more about these occupations. Talk to developers about their careers, use the resources of professional organizations, attend game and app development summer camps, participate in competitions, and most importantly, try to

The future is bright for game developers because there are so many different types of games to design (including car racing games, pictured here).

develop your own computer game or app. Who knows, maybe you'll create the next *Minecraft* or *Call of Duty*. Good luck on your career exploration!

TEXT-DEPENDENT QUESTIONS:

1. Why is demand growing for computer game and app developers?
2. Why do some women avoid pursuing careers in game and app development?
3. What factors could slow career growth?

RESEARCH PROJECT:

Spend some time exploring the future of computer game and app development. How will AI, virtual reality, and other technologies change the field? How will the work of developers change in the future? What tasks do you think will become automated? Write a report about your findings and present it to your class.

PHOTO CREDITS

FURTHER READING

Greer, Paul. *STEM Careers: A Student's Guide to Opportunities in Science, Technology, Engineering and Maths*. Bath, United Kingdom: Trotman Education, 2018.

Hansen, Dustin. *Game On!: Video Game History from Pong and Pac-Man to Mario, Minecraft, and More*. New York: Feiwel & Friends, 2016.

Hennessey, Jonathan, and Jack McGowan. *The Comic Book Story of Video Games: The Incredible History of the Electronic Gaming Revolution*. New York: Ten Speed Press, 2017.

Pearl, John. *Becoming a Video Game Artist: From Portfolio Design to Landing the Job*. Boca Raton, FL: CRC Press, 2016.

INTERNET RESOURCES

www.bls.gov/ooh/computer-and-information-technology/software-developers.htm: This section of the *Occupational Outlook Handbook* features information on job duties, educational requirements, salaries, and the employment outlook for software developers.

www.gamecareerguide.com: Visit this website to read article about game development and view samples of students' work.

www.careers.govt.nz/jobs-database/it-and-telecommunications/information-technology/game-developer: This website from the New Zealand government provides information on required skills, educational requirements, and job duties for game developers.

www.bls.gov/ooh/arts-and-design/multimedia-artists-and-animators.htm: Visit this website for job duties, educational requirements, salaries, and the employment outlook for multimedia artists and animators.

https://medium.com/cup-of-tea/working-in-games-4de9b0a5df7e: Designers and artists provide helpful advice about working in the gaming industry.

INDEX

EDUCATIONAL VIDEO LINKS

Chapter 1:

Learn what daily life is like for a video game designer: http://x-qr.net/1Kaq

An app developer discusses his work: http://x-qr.net/1K5q

Chapter 3:

Learn how students are earning money for college by participating in e-sports competitions: http://x-qr.net/1KJH

Chapter 4:

Learn about computer game development education programs at Academy of Art University: http://x-qr.net/1KTU

Chapter 5:

Eleven developers offer their predictions on the future of gaming: http://x-qr.net/1LMN

AUTHOR BIOGRAPHY

Andrew Morkes has been a writer and editor for more than twenty-five years. He is the author of more than twenty-five books about college-planning and careers, including all of the titles in this series, many titles in the Careers in the Building Trades series, the *Vault Career Guide to Social Media*, and *They Teach That in College!?: A Resource Guide to More Than 100 Interesting College Majors*, which was selected as one of the best books of the year by the library journal *Voice of Youth Advocates*. He is also the author and publisher of "The Morkes Report: College and Career Planning Trends" blog.